THE ADJUNCT
STUDY GUIDE

The Instructional Design Library

Volume 1

THE ADJUNCT STUDY GUIDE

Danny G. Langdon
Director of Instructional Design Research
The American College
Bryn Mawr, Pennsylvania

Danny G. Langdon
Series Editor

Educational Technology Publications
Englewood Cliffs, New Jersey 07632

Library of Congress Cataloging in Publication Data

Langdon, Danny G
　　The adjunct study guide.

　　(The Instructional design library; v. no. 1)
　　Bibliography: p.
　　1. Independent study. 2. Study, Method of.
I. Title. II. Series.
LB1049.L35　　378.1'7'943　　77-25457
ISBN 0-87778-105-2

Printed in the United States of America.

Library of Congress Catalog Card Number: 77-25457.

International Standard Book Number: 0-87778-105-2.

First Printing: February, 1978.

PREFACE

The Adjunct Study Guide grew out of a need to provide an effective study means for students who pursue learning on an independent, self-study basis. It was designed also to be just as effective for those using the Study Guide as a means of preparatory study prior to regular classroom instruction.

During the research, development, and repeated tryout for an effective study guide design, the need to provide confirming feedback (answers) to student responses presented a particular problem in need of a solution. Answers to questions were easy enough to provide, much the same as by various programmed instruction means—immediately following the question or on another page. At the same time, however, it became apparent that a means was necessary to further assist the student in tying these answers (and, therefore, the objectives) together so as to avoid individual answers existing in a vacuum. The result was the innovation of the Summary approach to providing confirming feedback. This is the most unique feature of the Adjunct Study Guide instructional design.

The author wishes to thank the many students and teachers of The American College who assisted him in developing this instructional design. In particular, the author owes a deep sense of gratitude to The American College for all its support and continuing interest in making learning research an easy task to pursue. Finally, thanks are due Ms. Laura Boornazian for her assistance in typing and editing this and the author's other manuscripts in this series.

v

CONTENTS

ABSTRACT

THE ADJUNCT STUDY GUIDE

The Adjunct Study Guide (ASG) is an effective means for guiding independent self-study, either as an instructional system itself or as preparatory study to classroom instruction. The adjunctive nature of the design provides a cost-effective means of providing instruction to students. Since the ASG is usually produced in written form, it can be easily distributed, generally at a low cost.

There are usually four to five major sections within the ASG. These include sections outlining the why of instruction, an overview of what is to be learned, specific outcomes and sources for learning, and a unique confirming-feedback and review system for student self-assessment of independent self-study progress. The ASG takes what is usually highly noninteractive learning sources (i.e., the typical textbook) and provides specific guidance and the opportunity to judge learning outcomes being achieved. The designer will find its application ranging mainly from the secondary school level to a variety of collegiate and training levels.

THE ADJUNCT
STUDY GUIDE

I.

USE

The Adjunct Study Guide (ASG) is most useful in meeting an instructional requirement in which there is complete independent student self-study, or where independent study is required as preparatory study to classroom instruction. The ASG is also useful when it is necessary, whether for financial or other reasons, that *existing* instructional materials be utilized. In this latter use, the ASG will be employed to tailor the existing materials to specific needs and for providing the learning effectiveness and efficiency that may be lacking in existing sources. Since cost implications—lack of money, personnel, or resources—often dictate what we can do when it comes to providing a more effective instructional mode for student learning needs, let us consider first how the ASG can be used to make more effective what we may already have on hand.

An Adjunct Study Guide is an instructional design that uses existing instructional or informational resources as key sources of content. The direction through and interaction with such sources are guided by the format of the study guide. Thus, the ASG can be made to be a necessary and integral part, along with existing resources, of learning experiences provided to students. A definition of a study guide must necessitate the use of the terms themselves, meaning a guide that directs student study. An *Adjunct*

Study Guide means a guide to instruction that does not contain all or possibly any of the content within itself, but rather *relies on external sources for the content of instruction*. According to Webster, an *adjunct* is *something joined or added to another thing but not essentially a part of it*. However, once you discover the utility of the ASG, it may well become much more than something *added on,* and indeed, quite essential to learning.

The ASG does not attempt to put all instructional materials physically together in one package, but utilizes a variety of instructional materials that already exist. The study guide is then a *map* that guides the student through content material. Any deficiencies in these materials—for instance, content areas that are found to be ineffective—are made up for by writing *new* and effective materials to be included physically within the study guide or as materials to be referenced by the study guide, but *located elsewhere*. An understanding of the deficiencies in most existing instructional materials will show why this *map*, in the form of an ASG, is useful. These deficiencies in particular are to be noted: lack of interaction, confirmation, and direction to critical content.

One of the missing features of most existing instructional materials is the lack of an interactive component which the student can use to actively judge his or her own progress in learning. Almost any textbook, for instance, will indicate this deficiency of interaction. This book itself lacks, for example, an opportunity for interaction, other than in a covert manner. Interaction means, in this sense, providing an opportunity to respond to questions representative of the intended goals and objectives which this book purports to have you achieve. This is said by no means to fix blame or fault on textbooks or other media resources that are noninteractive. Usually they are non-interactive because such sources are written to serve a multitude of needs, and the individual teacher or designer of instruction is left with the task of making the resource specific to students' needs, as he or she would have the students learn. The Adjunct Study Guide is a way of tailoring existing resources to specific needs, and doing so with interactive components which make instructional delivery more effective.

In addition to a general lack of interaction (usually through questions, although it might also mean carrying out activities, experiments, drawing, speaking, and so forth), existing resources for learning also lack a confirmation function following student responses. It is one thing, for instance, to add questions to be answered as one reads a textbook and writes answers, and it is another to know if such responding is *correct*. One might suppose that all that is needed are the questions to be answered; for, having written an answer, the student can go back into the text and find if he or she was right. The problem with this is that it is difficult for students to *find* if they are correct or incorrect. This is particularly true when they have responded incorrectly. Therefore, a source of correct answers is needed; a source to be used as a means of comparison between a student's answer and an acceptable, or criterion, answer. Confirmations (answers, if you will) to interaction *vis-a-vis* questions is important in improving the effectiveness of essentially non-interactive learning sources. Confirmation is also important in providing reinforcement. The ASG will help to provide both interaction and confirmation.

Finally, a third missing component of most existing instructional materials is a lack of clear directions to what is *critical* content. Existing sources usually contain much content we don't really want students to learn, or content that is simply outdated or out of the sequence desired. Deficiencies such as these are usually random and not confined to single chapters or segments. The ASG provides a convenient means for directing the student to exactly what we want him or her to look for or to avoid. It can be structured to allow for the addition of what is missing and in any sequence desired.

Therefore, in terms of making existing, non-interactive source materials more effective, the ASG is a cost-effective way of providing direction to critical content, giving missing interaction, and assuring correct confirmation of what is learned. By definition, then, an Adjunct Study Guide is an instructional design that provides direction, interaction, and confirming feedback to existing content sources made available to students as learning resources.

Now, if our existing instructional materials have these problems—lack of interaction, missing content, sequence problems, and outdated content—why not just write a whole new program to meet our needs? It usually boils down to a lack of time, money, and personnel, to do so. Besides, most existing resources are at least somewhat effective. It is really a question of how to make what exists *more effective* at a reasonable cost and with a minimum of developmental effort.

Beyond saving *production* costs and time, and improving the effectiveness of learning in general, the Adjunct Study Guide has two principal applications: (1) as a means of independent study, and (2) as a means of independent study to be augmented by other instruction, such as in-class lessons. For reasons that will be explained shortly, it is suggested that in approaching the development of an Adjunct Study Guide, the designer thinks in terms of its use as if it were to be employed solely for independent study—that it will not be augmented by in-class instruction. To understand why this approach to development is suggested, one must understand both the learning environment in which students are normally placed and certain motivational aspects behind their study.

First, an understanding of the student's learning environment is important, for it tells us something about the *degree*
of instruction that must be provided. The following will serve
as a general description of the environment in which we
usually find students.

Visualize the student as a lonely character, somewhere *out*
there on his or her own, about to enter a classroom. If we, as
teachers or designers of instruction, assume that student
study outside of a classroom is less important than what
occurs inside the classroom, then we are sacrificing both
some learning effectiveness and efficiency for ourselves as
teachers and for the students as learners. What typically
happens in classroom instruction is that we say to the
student, *You read or do this outside of class and then come*
to class and I'll go over the whole thing with you again. We
assume, in a sense, that students cannot learn most of what
we want them to learn outside the classroom; or, if we
assume they can learn outside, we do very little about it. If,
on the other hand, we did assume and *validate* certain
assumptions—that they could and do learn outside the
classroom—then the small amount of valuable time for
in-class activity could be devoted to truly crucial requirements. Some of this in-class time could be devoted to learner
objectives the students have not achieved outside the
classroom. What we might do is assess by pretesting what
they did not learn on the outside as a group or individually,
and work with them in the classroom either as a group or as
individuals.

The important point to be drawn from the discussion
above is that if the study guide instructional design is chosen
as a means to prescribe instruction, then in developing that
study guide, assume that you will try to teach *everything*
through use of the study guide, whether or not it is to be
augmented by classroom instruction.

Assume that the student, in using a study guide, is not going to come to class. Use classroom time, which is a rather short period, for purposes for which it is best suited. The classroom is most likely the only opportunity for the individual student to come and solve the *individual* content difficulties he or she is attempting to master. Another instructional design in this series, called the Construct Lesson Plan, will show how to maximize classroom instruction following independent study by students either through use of the ASG or other independent study means.

Why development should be viewed in this manner, as if we are serving the independent learner, can be further emphasized by looking also at student motivation toward study outside the classroom. If the students realize that the material learned outside the classroom will be rehashed again in class, then many of them do not sense any reason to engage in preparatory study. They draw the conclusion that they will *just take good notes in class.* Making the ASG a *necessary* part of the student's learning effort will then avoid the point of view that it is some kind of *supplement* to learning—which it certainly need not be.

Obviously, there is value in students coming together to share ideas, interpretations of content, and so forth. It is not being suggested here in any way that this activity be diminished or that it could be taken care of solely by independent study, using a study guide. Quite the contrary, what is being stressed is that *effective* study-guide learning can and will increase the potential of students to participate; to be more fully versed in content; and to engage in group activity on a higher and more desirable level.

The Adjunct Study Guide is an instructional design in which the maximum of independent study can be realized, whether augmented by subsequent classroom instruction or not. When a study guide is developed, it should be produced on the assumption that it will be used for complete, independent study, without benefit of subsequent classroom instruction.

Finally, if certain learning requirements are to be completed solely on the basis of independent self-study, then it is especially critical to let the students know exactly what is to be learned (the objectives) and, equally, they should *know* that they are learning on their own (through questions and answers). Such might be the case when a course is structured so that the majority of learning will be directed in the classroom, but certain additional requirements are expected to be met outside the classroom. More likely, however, independent self-study would be expected in situations where home study programs are necessary, or in many industrial situations where busy professionals are provided with self-study programs. Continuing education programs will find the ASG particularly useful. Many such continuing education programs must be administered on a decentralized basis, such as the *open learning* programs where much of learning is done at home, and the students are brought together for limited periods of time (or not at all) and must demonstrate learning by a final examination.

As a final note regarding the many uses to which an Adjunct Study Guide can be directed, it is important to understand that existing sources include the full range of content sources. This means not only textual materials, but also audio and visual means, the majority of which are usually non-interactive. The ASG can equally as well provide guidance through these learning resources. Thus, what is most effective can be used to its fullest advantage. Where ineffectiveness exists, new resources can easily be added or design features provided in the ASG which will make that which is essentially ineffective, effective. We shall now see *how*.

II.

OPERATIONAL DESCRIPTION

The Adjunct Study Guide is for student use. A student point of reference, therefore, will be taken in the description which follows. In this section, an overview of the ASG will be provided in terms of (1) the essential design features which are part of the ASG, and (2) how these design features work together. In the next section of this book, *Design Format,* a specific sample of the ASG will be given and detailed as an extension of the following overview.

The essential features to be found in the Adjunct Study Guide include:

1. Student learning is guided according to learner objectives, specific references, and sequence.

In the Use section of this book, the importance of providing direction to *critical* content was stressed. You will recall that this design is used primarily for guiding independent self-study. In this use, clear and concise direction to learning outcomes for the student is highly important. Clear and concise direction is important since there is no one, such as a teacher, along the path of learning to straighten out misguided direction on the student's part. Learner objectives will be the primary means of providing clear and concise direction. Why objectives? The answer lies in viewing the student's problem when guided by the more typical means of *content headings.*

Most existing learning resources are structured around content headings. For example, this book is structured in this manner. You know that you are reading under the heading of *Operational Description*. This heading, however, does not tell you exactly what you are to derive from your reading. The problem with content headings is that they don't really indicate the outcome of what is to be learned by reading the information placed under the heading—unless, of course, we assume that everything under such a content heading is to be learned. This *is* the case, or at least my intent, in regard to this book.

However, as often as not, many of the sources we provide students contain many more things than we wish them to gain a mastery of, or indeed, lack the things we want, or are partially ineffective in communicating. Even if a resource does contain everything we want of students, there are different ways of expressing what is wanted. What does all this mean? Here is an example.

In a chemistry course there is a segment of learning concerned with Boyle's Law. This law deals with the relationship between pressure, volume, and temperature of substances in a gaseous state. Let us suppose that the content source is a chemistry textbook. In this text the content covers what is meant by each of these factors, how they relate, how they can be determined, how to calculate problems based upon knowing two of these factors, and the relationship to other laws of chemistry. Now, unless we want all of these things learned, as teachers and designers of instruction we must decide which of these *outcomes* students are to master, and as a result provide direction in statements which tell the students in what terms these outcomes are to be expressed. For instance, rather than merely saying to the student, *Study Boyle's Law*, the learner objective for this content might be confined to the following: *Using Boyle's*

Law, calculate problems involving temperature, volume, and pressure of gaseous substances. You can see from this that learner objectives make the task of communicating outcomes much easier; and, for the self-studier using an ASG, communicating outcomes is crucial.

Direction to learning requirements is controlled in the ASG by more than providing objectives or content headings.

Direction is also provided by informing the student what he or she is to read, hear, or view. In the ASG, direction by references to sources is done on a specific basis—pages to read in a text, for example. Such references will immediately follow and be referenced to specific objectives.

Direction is also typically guided by a third factor, in addition to objectives and references. This is a certain sequence of the objectives. As you will discover in looking at a specific example of the ASG in the next section, on *Design Format*, the objectives will be placed in a predetermined sequence. However, there will be some flexibility by using an objectives-based approach. The given sequence will allow the student to proceed in a different manner if he or she so chooses.

Finally, a fourth kind of direction is provided in the ASG. This is the direction which says why a student should study a particular module or segment of learner objectives. We shall identify this type of direction to learning as the Purpose and Significance. It includes considerations related to providing an overview of content prior to learning specific objectives and why the content is important.

    2. Content, in addition to the existing resources, will usually be required and can be incorporated into the Study Guide itself.

The instructional means addressed in this book are composed of two overall parts. One is the existing instructional and informational sources, and the other is the

Adjunct Study Guide itself. The existing sources would include such things as textbooks, films, library materials, audio programs, videotapes, operations manuals, computer programs, and even resource persons. The author has characterized these resources as being non-interactive (usually)—that is, without directions (objectives), interaction (questions), and confirmation (answers). The Adjunct Study Guide contains all those things—directions, interaction, and confirmation—that the existing sources do not generally contain. In regard to the existing sources themselves, it is sometimes the case that any or all of the following exists:

1. Some parts of the existing sources are ineffective in content treatment.
2. Some parts of the existing sources are outdated.
3. Some parts of the existing sources are missing—that is, what we want to exist, simply does not; or, more likely, it exists in another source that for one reason or another (such as cost) we cannot provide to all students.

The dilemma with existing sources is as follows. We have sources that will present content, for the most part, but what do we do about ineffective, missing, or outdated portions of the existing content? In using an Adjunct Study Guide, the answer lies in incorporating into the guide the missing content, or content that is more effective or that updates the outmoded content. There is a specific segment in the Adjunct Study Guide where this can be done. Therefore, *other* content sources would include that which is within the body of the ASG itself, as well as the content which is external to it.

Before moving to the next essential feature of an ASG, let us expand on the topic of the existing sources. It is probably true that the existing sources to be used will generally be in the form of a written text or texts. This is due to cost and ease-of-distribution factors. It is important to realize, however, that existing sources may include any of the content materials that can be made available to students. Indeed, if it is possible, a duplication of resources in the same medium (i.e., two texts) or different media (i.e., a text and an audio program) can be referenced in the ASG. The designer might well list multiple sources in terms of the *primary* sources and *supplementary* sources. This provides the advantage of allowing students to choose what source they prefer, or to study different resources to the point that they feel they have mastered an objective(s), or to study a primary source and to use the supplementary source for remedial purposes.

The ASG will allow the designer to include resources that he or she might not otherwise think of using. For example, newspaper clippings and articles from journals are often good sources of content. In sum, the ASG allows the designer to pick and choose from a variety of existing sources and to find sources that seem to be the most effective. Those that prove upon actual use not to be effective can then be eliminated, and others chosen or written into the study guide itself. Revision, you will find, is a fairly easy matter in the ASG approach, and therefore becomes one of its major advantages from a design standpoint.

   3. The ASG has a means for structuring interaction that is usually missing from existing sources so that the student can assess his or her own learning.

Interaction usually takes the form of questions, although it may also include tasks and activities of a larger nature which call for student involvement. It has already been emphasized that, next to a lack of direction, interaction is the component usually missing from existing sources of learning materials. Our thinking as to what will be needed for interaction must be guided by the direction—the objectives—we establish. In other words, if we tell the student, *Here is an objective to be achieved* (which is the first requirement stated above), and,

Here are the resources to help you achieve (which is the second requirement stated above), then we need something which the student can use to find out that he or she has learned the objective as a result of using the resources. This sounds so easy and necessary, but how often have you seen the interaction missing, or found interaction that is something other than what the objectives specified?

Two levels of interaction will be suggested for the ASG. The first level is that type of interaction which *helps* the student to achieve an objective. We call the questions used in this regard *enabling questions*. The second type of interaction is that which provides the opportunity to perform the objective as it is stated. We call this *criterion questioning*. An easy way to distinguish between enabling and criterion questioning is that an enabling question is a *piece* of an objective, while a criterion question is the *whole* of an objective.

An enabling question to the objective previously given on Boyle's Law would be:

When applying Boyle's Law, which value is held constant?

This question, you can surmise, would help the student check his or her understanding of one part of the objective. The criterion question to the objective would be one involving the calculation (as the objective states), such as:

> *If 40 liters of gas at 760 mm of pressure, held at a constant temperature is changed to a pressure of 1,520 mm, what would be the resulting volume?*

Additional examples to clarify the difference between enabling and criterion questioning will be provided in an example in the *Design Format* section of this book.

> *4. Finally, a means of confirmation to the interaction is provided so that the students will know the correctness or incorrectness of their responses.*

Confirmations are answers to the enabling and criterion

questions. The particular instructional design format for the ASG provides a unique way of *delivering* confirmation such that added benefits, including review and interrelating objectives learned, are provided as well.

Having the above overview of essential features behind us, let us view the Adjunct Study Guide in terms of student use. First, the student is informed in a descriptive manner why he or she is studying a selected segment, module, or unit of instruction. This includes an account of the purpose and significance of that which he or she is about to enter into, so that some initial appreciation can be gained for generating interest and motivation. Obviously, one cannot rely solely on this to maintain interest and motivation, but such an introductory set of statements is a good starting point. In addition to describing the purpose and significance, a general view of outcomes to be derived as a result of the study of the unit of instruction is also provided in terms of what will be labeled as goals. Goals are similar to objectives, except they can be measured less directly than objectives and are usually stated in broad terms. The difference between the two becomes more evident in the example provided in the next section, on *Design Format.*

Following the statements on purpose, significance, and goals is a content outline. This is given for a general overview of a unit of instruction. While the content outline may sound repetitious of the purpose, significance, and goals statements, it is not—in the sense that the outline is a thumbnail overview of content and how it relates, while goals are more *outcome oriented.* Statements of purpose, significance, goals, and content overview may seem like a great deal of material, but we shall see that in the ASG these are confined generally to about three pages, and are easily reviewed in a matter of minutes by the student.

Immediately following the above *introductory* remarks,

the student then enters into the activity of learning toward specific outcomes to be achieved from a unit of instruction. This is accomplished according to the following procedure.

First, the student is provided an objective to read. This is found within the context of a content heading which comes from the Content Outline that has previously been reviewed by the student. Thus, the specific objective which the student is about to study is *seen in light of its overall relationship to a unit or module of instruction.*

Having read an objective, the student has two specific pieces of vital information to consider. He or she knows what content is to be learned and in what manner mastery of the objective must be expressed. Let us take the previously given objective and see what this means. The objective was:

> *Using Boyle's Law, calculate problems involving temperature, volume, and pressure of gaseous substances.*

The content of the above objective is: *problems involving temperature, volume, and pressure of gaseous substances.*

In effect, this tells the student to look, as he or she reads, listens, or hears from the existing sources provided, for these content topics. This is the *content direction* provided by the objective. But the objective also tells the student what must be done with this content. He or she must *calculate* problems—perform mathematical relationships. The *outcome* of the learning is specific and measurable. It does not say to simply "study Boyle's Law," or to do something else, like give a definition, identify the factors involved, or some other kind of outcome. Of course, the student may need to learn many of these latter outcomes in order to finally perform the calculation, but the *principal* outcome is the calculation itself.

Following the statement of an objective which the student has read, the reference or references to existing sources are listed. These can be used to *learn* about the objective. The nature of the reference, whatever source it might be, is provided on a specific basis. Rather than specifying, for instance, *Read Chapter 4 in the O'Malley text*, a reference is usually given to specific pages, like *Read pages 78-80.*

Furthermore, if for some reason there is something in the reading that need be excluded, then the reference may be followed by a statement of what can be excluded, i.e., *Read pages 78-80; however, the discussion on the historical background of Boyle's discovery may be excluded.* This is not to suggest, however, that such specific exclusions be made if for some reason it is important that the student also read what doesn't relate right now but will be used later. It may be that the historical background is a part of a subsequent objective.

Following the reference to the existing resource(s), there may be included a specific section on *additional* content. This would be necessary in instances where there is a lack of clarity in the existing reading, or there is missing or outdated content. In the ASG this is usually provided for by adding such content immediately following the specified outside references. This could include content descriptions as well as additional examples and illustrations. For the moment, understand that additional content can be added to the ASG, and that it usually follows the references provided to existing sources.

Thus far, the following sequence has been detailed for the ASG:

1. Purpose, Significance, Goals.
2. Content Outline.
3. A specific objective, followed by reference to existing sources, and possibly additional content contained within the study guide itself.

There are two remaining parts to follow.

As a generalization, we might say that, having gone through the reference sources, the student has learned the objective(s) studied. We, as instructional designers, might make such a conclusion, but it would be far better for each individual student to conclude this for himself or herself. Of course, we must recognize also that some learning requirements (objectives) require practice and application to conclude that learning has indeed taken place.

It is not such a simple matter to conclude that because someone read, they have also *learned*. It is amazing, however, how often we do so.

If we can suppose that the student has proceeded through the reference sources and activities, and has done what has been asked, then the next step in the ASG is to provide the means for him or her to demonstrate mastery. Now, because the ASG is usually for content related learning, this *demonstration of mastery* will usually take the form of questions which the student will answer. The questions will immediately follow the reference to content, or if additional content is written in the study guide, then immediately following the additional content. These questions may be ones that aid in student learning, which were labeled earlier as enabling questions, and will certainly include questions requiring demonstration of the mastery of an objective as it is stated. The latter is exemplified by the question which called for a calculation of given figures in the Boyle's Law objective. This was labeled as a criterion question. The objective called for calculations, and the criterion question(s) would demand the same, equal response.

Once the student has responded to the questions provided for an objective, he or she can judge the accuracy of responses by answers to the questions that are provided in the study guide. When the *Design Format* is described shortly, you will find that these answers may be placed right after the questions, on the same page, on the next page, or elsewhere in what will become identified as the Summary to the ASG.

Finally, from an operational standpoint, there may be need for other learning requirements to follow the basic mastery of the objectives of a module of instruction. The *Design Format* section will illustrate this type of *cumulative* application, plus additional considerations that can be provided.

In concluding the description of the operational features of the Adjunct Study Guide, it probably goes without saying that what has been described thus far is no less than what we would expect in any instructional design. The ASG, however, has some unique features for providing and guiding these instructional requirements and needs. For instance, the manner in which confirmations will be provided will achieve a dual function of confirmation and follow-up review. The flexibility to add new sources of content within the ASG will provide many benefits in improving overall learning effectiveness.

You should have sensed from the foregoing operational description that the ASG provides a logical order to learning in these stages: introductory, to specific, to summary learning. The introductory phase is achieved on both a *why* and a *what* basis. Statements of purpose and significance are read by the student so that he or she can gain an appreciation of why the material is to be studied. Then, statements of goals are given as an overview of general learning outcomes to be achieved. Goals are followed by a content outline, which serves to give the student a content overview in light of the purpose, significance, and goals. Then, from this introduction, specific learning is guided by learner objectives, to which existing reference sources are keyed; and possibly other content sources are contained in the Study Guide itself.

Questions to the objectives are asked, and the student's written responses can be checked against answers provided. At the end of the specific learning is a Summary section, which serves to tie together the several objectives learned into a unit; it provides a summary for later review study.

A key point to keep in mind is that the Adjunct Study Guide is an instructional design used to take what is non-interactive in the way of existing instructional materials, and to make these existing sources interactive and more directive for clear, effective communication to students. In this sense, then, the ASG can be viewed as providing guidance for effective learning between the student and the existing sources selected for him or her. This is done so that the student can follow his or her own course of independent self-study, which may or may not be followed by other means of study, such as in the classroom.

III.

DESIGN FORMAT

You will find within this section, in Figures 1 through 5, a complete sample of the Adjunct Study Guide for one assignment of an introductory economics course. The description which follows will detail the specific format of the ASG and will use the sample for illustrative purposes. It is suggested that you peruse the general layout before reading further, particularly Figures 1, 2, 3.1, 4.1, and 5.1.

The illustrative ASG shown here is composed of five sections. Four of these sections are used in most learning applications. Additional sections, such as the fifth section to be illustrated here, can be added to meet specific learning requirements (i.e., cumulative study, review, remediation, etc.). The four required sections of an Adjunct Study Guide include:

- *Purpose, Significance, and Goals*
- *Content Outline*
- *Objective-Reference-Question*
- *Summary*

The fifth section to be illustrated is the:

- *Cumulative Problem*

Each section will be described separately. It is necessary to emphasize, however, that each section is a building block to the next section. No single section should be viewed as standing alone. After this initial description, we shall see how

Figure 1

HS 304   ASSIGNMENT 5

ECONOMICS   SECTION I

THEORY OF NATIONAL INCOME DETERMINATION
(CONCLUDED)

PURPOSE

This assignment continues to explore the theory of income determination which was introduced in Assignment 4. The basic tools and concepts which were mastered there are examined more thoroughly, and the role of government is introduced.

SIGNIFICANCE

At this point, several applications of economic tools should become apparent, and the student should be using them with increasing frequency as a basis for making judgments about national economic policies.

GOALS

1. To understand how shifts in investment and consumption schedules affect national income and vice versa.

2. To understand how government expenditure and tax policies may be used to close inflationary and deflationary gaps.

TEXT REFERENCE

Samuelson—Chapter 13

Summary Begins on Page 5.16

each section relates to the others for guiding effective learning on an independent self-study basis.

Purpose-Significance-Goals

As with most instructional designs, units of objectives to be learned are organized around modules, assignments, or specific lessons. Here we will refer to them as assignments. Usually assignments are organized according to major content or task subjects. In the illustration given here, in Figure 1, the assignment is from an economics course, and is concerned with the *Theory of National Income Determination.*

The introduction to assignments structured on the ASG is always a series of statements designed to achieve two basic aims. First, we have some indication of what the assignment is about, and secondly, why it is important in the overall course of study. The first aim is labeled the Goals, and the second the Purpose and Significance. In specifying and writing each, these aims become somewhat intertwined.

Figure 1, for example, illustrates how the Purpose and Significance provided descriptive information of the sort mentioned above as the aims. It is generally a two-page-or-less description of what the lesson is about and why it is important in relation to its eventual use or study as an *academic* generalization, or in relation to other courses of study, or other similar purposes which answer the question *WHY?* You will observe, in the example, statements about economics, what the content is in general, and why it is important. The content is described in both the purpose and the generic goals statements. These goals, by the way, are not specific, behaviorally-defined objectives. The specific objectives in a subsequent major section of the ASG will reflect an extension of these goals. Thus, the goals may be viewed in a number of ways:

1. They provide an overview of content.

2. They will be achieved by learning the specific objectives
   and the lesson as a unit.
3. They help to relate, on a general basis, the study of one
   assignment to others and the program of study (i.e.,
   economics) in general.

Following the Purpose-Significance-Goals section is a
listing of the existing reference sources that will be used in
the assignment. You will also note, in Figure 1, a statement
at the bottom of the page which refers the student to where
the *Summary* is to be found. Later we will return to the use
of this statement.

Content Outline

Figure 2 illustrates a typical Content Outline used in the
ASG. There is nothing unique about the layout or intent of
this section of the ASG. It is structured like many such
content outlines that you have seen previously.

The reasons for providing a Content Outline are twofold.
First, it provides a generic content overview of the assignment. It is, in this sense, an extension of the statements of
the Purpose-Significance-Goals from the previous section.
The difference here lies in being able to see how the content
relates to other material. Also, the content is presented in
more detail. No emphasis is given in the outline, however, to
the outcomes to be achieved from seeing this content, as in
the case of the goals and in the objecitves which are to
follow.

Secondly, the Content Outline will serve a functional aim.
It helps keep the student oriented as to where and what he or
she is going to be studying and learning. Since, in the next
section, student study is guided on an objective by objective
basis, the Content Outline will be used with the objectives to
help keep the learning of individual objectives in overall
perspective. If the outline is not provided, then overall study

Figure 2

THEORY OF NATIONAL INCOME DETERMINATION
(CONCLUDED)

OUTLINE OF SUBJECT MATTER

1. Investment and income (S 234-240)

   a. How shifts in the consumption schedule affect income
   b. The difference between autonomous and induced investment
   c. The paradox of thrift

2. Deflationary and inflationary gaps (S 240-243)

   a. Measurement of deflationary and inflationary gaps
   b. Demand-pull inflation

3. Fiscal policy in income determination (S 243-246)

   a. Government spending policies
   b. Government tax policies

might seem fragmented. It will be easier to understand the nature of this orientation process when the next section, on Objectives and Questions, is reviewed. You will then find the content of this Content Outline used again in relation to the specific objectives.

In sum, the Content Outline provides an overview of what is to be learned from a content standpoint and helps to keep the learning of specific objectives in context.

Objective-Reference-Question

Section III, Objective-Reference-Question, is divided into three major parts and includes two other parts of some lesser importance. Figures 3.1 through 3.13 are illustrations of Section III for the objectives of the economics assignment. You can see that this section is generally the longest of all sections in the ASG. As the title of this section indicates, the three major parts are the Objective, Reference, and Question(s).

Having read the Purpose-Significance-Goals (Section I) and the Content Outline (Section II), the student proceeds through Section III as follows:

1. Beginning at the top of the page, the student first sees a content heading. For instance, in Figure 3.1, you see the title of the assignment and a major heading, *Investment and Income*, which was drawn from the Content Outline of Section II. The purpose of the content heading is simply one of letting the student know where the objective he or she is about to learn falls within the overall content of the total assignment. The next two objectives, Figures 3.2 and 3.3, also fall within the same topic, while the objective in Figure 3.4 begins a new topic.

2. Next, the student reads the objective he or she is to learn. The objective provides direction to what is to

be learned—a target of learning to be hit, so to speak.

3. Next, the student notes a reference to an existing content source to read; or it might be a film to view, a tape to hear, or some other content resource available. Directions given here might even include what the student should not have to pay attention to within the assigned reference.

4. A space for Notes is provided so that the student can record any special notes he or she might want for future reference in reviewing the assignment. The notes section may be of additional value to students who would be using this ASG as preparatory study to classroom instruction. Additional notes can be added as the objective is reviewed with a teacher in class.

5. Having finished reading the content, the student then answers a question or series of questions related to the objective he or she is studying. Later in this description, we'll return to the types of questions that should be included here.

6. Having written his or her answer to the question(s), the student is provided a confirming answer in the study guide with which he or she can compare his or her own written answer. Usually, this answer is to be found in Section IV—The Summary—of the Adjunct Study Guide, although for some types of questions, the answer may be found directly following the question on the same or next page. The distinction as to where the answer is to be located will be elaborated upon shortly.

One of the first things you should have noted about the above layout is that all references are to existing instructional materials. In this case, the Samuelson economics text is the primary source of existing content. In Figure 3.1, you will note that a specific reference has been given to pay special attention to a figure in the text itself. Furthermore, Figure 3.13 shows a reference made to a previously learned objective in order to emphasize the interrelationship of one objective to another. Other common things to be done with the reference include: (1) telling the student what reading materials he or she could exclude within a reading reference, such as outdated facts and figures or historical background information that simply isn't necessary or that might be referred to later in another objective; or (2) if additional content is needed, but is not included in the existing reference sources, a new part can be added to Section III. While this addition is not illustrated in this particular economics assignment, in that the text used contains sufficient content coverage for the objectives given, it will be easy to describe what is to be done for content that is missing from an existing reference. There is nothing to preclude writing your own content within the Study Guide itself. Assuming the content is not too long, it can be written immediately following the Reference part of Section III, under the title, *Additional Content.* If the additional content is rather long, you might prefer to include it as one piece at the end of the assignment and make reference to it in the Reference section. This is particularly wise where the specific content is for use with more than one objective in an Assignment or between several Assignments.

The time saved in utilizing existing reference materials that you know work through validation, augmented by the addition of sources you develop on your own, should clearly speak for the cost-savings benefit in utilizing an adjunctive instructional design such as the ASG. In addition, it allows the designer to tailor-make a course of study to student needs around materials that best serve the students and that can be easily up-dated.

(text continued on page 44)

Figure 3.1

HS 304   ASSIGNMENT 5

ECONOMICS   SECTION III

THEORY OF NATIONAL INCOME DETERMINATION (CONCLUDED)

INVESTMENT AND INCOME

#1   *Objective*   Describe the effect on national income when sched-
                     uled saving shifts upward and scheduled investment
                     remains constant.

      Reference   Samuelson pages 235-236 and Figure 13.2 on page
                     236

      Notes

      Question   If saving shifts upward and investment remains
                     constant, what will happen to national income?

      Answer   CHECK SUMMARY ITEM #1

Figure 3.2

ASSIGNMENT 5   HS 304

SECTION III   ECONOMICS

**THEORY OF NATIONAL INCOME DETERMINATION
(CONCLUDED)**

INVESTMENT AND INCOME

#2   *Objective*   Distinguish between "autonomous" investment and "induced" investment.

     Reference   Samuelson page 237

     Notes

     Question   What is the difference between "autonomous" investment and "induced" investment?

     Answer   CHECK SUMMARY ITEM #2

Figure 3.3

HS 304   ASSIGNMENT 5

ECONOMICS   SECTION III

THEORY OF NATIONAL INCOME DETERMINATION
(CONCLUDED)

INVESTMENT AND INCOME

#3   *Objective*   Define the term "paradox of thrift," and explain how
                    thriftiness affects national income (a) at a depressed
                    level and (b) at an inflated level.

      Reference   Samuelson pages 237-239

      Notes

      Question   A.   What is the "paradox of thrift"?

                    B.   How does thriftiness affect national income
                          (1)   at a depressed level

                          (2)   at an inflated level

      Answer   CHECK SUMMARY ITEM #3

Figure 3.4

ASSIGNMENT 5   HS 304

SECTION III   ECONOMICS

**THEORY OF NATIONAL INCOME DETERMINATION
(CONCLUDED)**

DEFLATIONARY AND INFLATIONARY GAPS

#4   *Objective*   Define the term "deflationary gap," and explain how
                   a deflationary gap affects income.

     Reference   Samuelson pages 240-241

     Notes

     Question   A.   What is a deflationary gap?

                  B.   How does a deflationary gap affect income?

     Answer   CHECK SUMMARY ITEM #4

Figure 3.5

HS 304   ASSIGNMENT 5

ECONOMICS   SECTION III

THEORY OF NATIONAL INCOME DETERMINATION
(CONCLUDED)

DEFLATIONARY AND INFLATIONARY GAPS

#5   *Objective*   Identify the formula and effect of prices of an "inflationary gap."

Reference   Samuelson pages 241-242

Notes

Question   An "inflationary gap" is

..... A.   an excess of C + I spending over GNP at full employment and causes prices to fall.

..... B.   an excess of S over I at full employment and causes prices to rise.

..... C.   an excess of GNP over C + I spending at full employment and causes prices to rise.

..... D.   an excess of I over S at full employment and causes prices to rise.

..... E.   an excess of C + S over C + I at full employment and causes prices to rise.

Answer   The correct choice is D.
For further clarification, CHECK SUMMARY ITEM #5

Figure 3.6

ASSIGNMENT 5   HS 304

SECTION III   ECONOMICS

THEORY OF NATIONAL INCOME DETERMINATION (CONCLUDED)

DEFLATIONARY AND INFLATIONARY GAPS

#6   *Objective*   Explain how deflationary and inflationary gaps are measured.

Reference   Samuelson pages 240-241

Notes

Question   How are deflationary and inflationary gaps measured?

Answer   CHECK SUMMARY ITEM #6

Figure 3.7

HS 304   ASSIGNMENT 5

ECONOMICS   SECTION III

THEORY OF NATIONAL INCOME DETERMINATION (CONCLUDED)

DEFLATIONARY AND INFLATIONARY GAPS

#7   *Objective*   Using 45-degree line diagrams, illustrate (a) a deflationary gap, and (b) an inflationary gap.

Reference   Samuelson pages 240-241 and Figures 13.5 and 13.6 on pages 240-241 .

Notes

Question   A.   Using the 45-degree line diagram below, draw and label a deflationary gap.

B.   Using the 45-degree line diagram below, draw and label an inflationary gap.

Answer   CHECK SUMMARY ITEM #7

Figure 3.8

ASSIGNMENT 5   HS 304

SECTION III   ECONOMICS

**THEORY OF NATIONAL INCOME DETERMINATION
(CONCLUDED)**

DEFLATIONARY AND INFLATIONARY GAPS

#8   *Objective*   Explain the term "demand-pull inflation."

Reference   Samuelson pages 241-242

Notes

Question   What does the term "demand-pull inflation" mean?

Answer   CHECK SUMMARY ITEM #8

Figure 3.9

HS 304   ASSIGNMENT 5

ECONOMICS   SECTION III

THEORY OF NATIONAL INCOME DETERMINATION
(CONCLUDED)

FISCAL POLICY

#9   *Objective*   Explain the purpose of fiscal policy.

     Reference   Samuelson page 243

     Notes

     Question   A.   What does the term "fiscal policy" mean?

                  B.   What is the purpose of "fiscal policy"?

     Answers   A.   Fiscal Policy is the general name given to
                      government and expenditure policy.

                 B.   CHECK SUMMARY ITEM #9

Figure 3.10

ASSIGNMENT 5   HS 304

SECTION III   ECONOMICS

THEORY OF NATIONAL INCOME DETERMINATION
(CONCLUDED)

FISCAL POLICY

#10 *Objective* Given a 45-degree line diagram, explain the change in
equilibrium level when "G" is added to "C" and "I."

References Samuelson page 243 and Figure 13.7 on page 243

Notes

Questions A. Write the correct word meaning for each of the
following symbols:
G = ...
C = ...
I = ...

B. C + I + G = _____

C. Using the 45-degree line diagram below, explain
what happens to equilibrium when "G" is
added to "C + I."

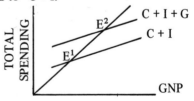

Answers A. G = Government expenditures on goods and services
C = Consumption expenditures
I = Private investment expenditures

B. GNP

C. CHECK SUMMARY ITEM #10

Figure 3.11

HS 304   ASSIGNMENT 5

ECONOMICS   SECTION III

THEORY OF NATIONAL INCOME DETERMINATION (CONCLUDED)

FISCAL POLICY

#11 *Objective* Assuming that all other factors remain constant, (a) explain the effect on national income of an increase in government expenditure, and (b) explain the effect on both national and disposable income of an increase or decrease in taxes.

Reference Samuelson pages 244-245

Notes

Question A. How is national income affected when all factors are held constant and only government expenditures are increased?

B. How is both disposable and national income affected when all factors are held constant and

   (1) only taxes are increased

   (2) only taxes are decreased

Answer CHECK SUMMARY ITEM #11

Figure 3.12

ASSIGNMENT 5   HS 304

SECTION III   ECONOMICS

THEORY OF NATIONAL INCOME DETERMINATION
(CONCLUDED)

FISCAL POLICY

#12 *Objective*   Given the necessary information, calculate the in-
crease in personal income tax required to reduce the
inflationary gap.

Reference   Samuelson pages 244-245

Notes

Question   If MPC for the economy is 2/3 and an inflationary
gap of $20 billion exists, what increase in personal
income taxes is needed to eliminate this gap?

Answer   CHECK SUMMARY ITEM #12

Figure 3.13

THEORY OF NATIONAL INCOME DETERMINATION
(CONCLUDED)

FISCAL POLICY

#13 *Objective* Given a sample situation, calculate the change in national income that would result from a concurrent increase in both taxes and government expenditures.

Reference Samuelson pages 244-245 and Assignment 5, Objective 11

Notes

Question Assuming an MPC of 2/3, what change in national income would result from a $20 billion increase in government expenditures financed by a new $20 billion increase in taxes?

Answer CHECK SUMMARY ITEM #13

Advantages of the suggested approach for Section III of the ASG include the following:

1. An objective by objective approach which allows for the clear delineation and communication of what is to be learned. The reader should observe that the objectives, not the content resources, define what is to be learned. For the self-studier, this is highly important for clear communication in a learning effort that for the most part must be pursued on his or her own.

2. Only those content sources needed should be referenced, thus saving valuable student study time.

3. Additional content sources can be added directly within the Study Guide wherein they relate and would be used.

4. The objectives and questions are together, so that the objectives can be readily at hand to the student in helping to guide his or her learning. Often as not, the objectives and questions are separated in many instructional designs. For instance, objectives are placed in an introduction. By the time the student gets to the source of content and the questions which he or she will use to check mastery of the objectives, the objectives have been forgotten. In the ASG, objectives and related questions are together.

5. Since students often like to keep notes for later reference, notes should be integrated with the objectives to which they are related. Also, as previously mentioned, should classroom instruction follow the use of the ASG, additional notes from the classroom discussion can be added in this same space.

The Summary

The fourth major section of the Adjunct Study Guide, the

Summary, serves two unique functions. Figures 4.1 through 4.5 illustrate a typical Summary.

You will first note, in Figure 4.1, that the Summary provides the answers (confirmations) to the questions the student had answered in the Section III. Here, in Figure 4.1, you see the answers to the questions for objectives 1 and 2. You will also note that the answers in the Summary are blocked off between parallel lines across the page. Furthermore, these answers are identified by the corresponding question number which the statement answers. Thus, when the student writes his or her answer to question #1 in Section III, he or she then looks in the Summary for the number one and finds a representative answer against which to compare his or her own written answer. Once the student has confirmed his or her own written answer, he or she then proceeds to the next objective and reference source (i.e., objective #2) in Section III; reads it; answers the question(s); checks the confirmation in the Summary; and so on, until all objectives have been completed and responded to. Note for now that only the answers in the Summary are blocked off and that there is additional content, in some instances, provided between answers.

Once all the questions in Section III have been answered and these answers have been checked in the Summary, the second function of the Summary becomes evident, and that is as a *summary*. By reading the Summary *after* completing all the objectives, references, and questions of the assignment, the student can read and tie together all the previously answered questions to objectives. In this use, it is like a summary that might be found at the end of a chapter in a textbook. Essentially, it ties together, in a most direct manner, that which has been learned. This is one extra (but most effective) means of tying instruction together beyond that which is normally done by the sequence in which the objectives are learned. The sequence of the reading material also aids in this same function. The Summary thus provides both feedback in terms of confirmations and a review of what has been learned, in a well integrated and straight-forward manner.

Here are some important points to be understood about what goes into and what should be excluded from the Summary:

1. The Summary is made up of answers to questions that test the objectives directly. We often call these kinds of questions criterion or terminal questions. By contrast, background questions, or what we often call enabling questions that aid in progressing toward successful mastery of criterion questions, are not confirmed in the Summary. For example, in Figure 3.10, you will note that three questions are asked. These are labeled questions A, B, and C. Note carefully that only question C is a question that calls for performance that is exactly the same as the objective. This question we would call a criterion question, in that it measures the criterion originally set forth—that is, the objective. Correspondingly, the answer to this question (as indicated at the bottom of the page) is placed in the Summary (see Summary Item #10 in Figure 4.4). Compare this, on the other hand, to questions A and B in Figure 3.10. These two questions are merely parts which aid or help (thus the name *enabling* questions) the student to answer the criterion question. If the student were unable to answer these enabling questions, he or she could not in all likelihood answer the criterion question. He or she is aware, then, that further study is needed before attempting to answer the criterion question(s). The point to be made at this time, however, is that the

(text continued on page 52)

Figure 4.1

ASSIGNMENT 5   HS 304

SECTION IV   ECONOMICS

**THEORY OF NATIONAL INCOME DETERMINATION
(CONCLUDED)**

SUMMARY

....

Investment and Income
In the previous assignment, the intersection of the saving and
investment schedules, and the intersection of C + I and the
45-degree line, were both identified as the equilibrium point
toward which national income would tend to gravitate. Also, the
multiplier doctrine was introduced, and the multiplier effect on
income resulting from a change in the level of investment was
illustrated. The multiplier also applies to shifts in the saving and
consumption schedules. A shift in a schedule means a change in
the desire to save or consume at all levels of income.

....
#1   When there is an upward shift of the saving schedule, with
       investment remaining constant, national income will fall, in a
       multiplier way, until a new income equilibrium point is reached.

....
       The desire to save more, illustrated by the upward shift in the
       saving schedule, results in a saving level that is not more than, but
       only equivalent to, the previous level because the level of
       investment has not increased by the same amount as saving.
       National income, therefore, will gravitate toward the equilibrium
       point where saving and investment are equal once more.

....
#2   Up to this point investment schedules have always been drawn
       parallel to the horizontal GNP axis, implying that investment is
       autonomous—independent of any change in income, output, or
       general economic activity. Actually, increases in income, output,
       or economic activity can stimulate higher levels of investment.
       For example, a rise in national income can result in higher
       consumption spending and consequently higher investment. This

Figure 4.2

HS 304   ASSIGNMENT 5

ECONOMICS   SECTION IV

stimulated investment, called induced investment, is graphically
illustrated by an upward-sloping line.

....

The graphic portrayal of induced investment is helpful in
demonstrating the paradox of thrift.

....

#3   The paradox of thrift is the proposition that if *people as a group*
     try to increase their saving they will end up saving less. The
     conclusion of the paradox is that an increase in saving may be
     desirable for an individual, but not necessarily for an entire
     economy.

     An upward shift in the saving schedule will result in reduced
     national income. However, because induced investment slopes
     downward with decreasing income, the new equilibrium level of
     national income will occur at a point where the new saving level is
     below the original saving level. The desire to save more results in
     saving less.

     Thriftiness has a different impact, depending on whether the
     economy is at an inflated level or a deflated level. During periods
     of inflation, an increase in thriftiness (reduced consumption) can
     reduce inflationary pressures. However, during depressed eco-
     nomic periods, the increased desire to save may depress the
     economy even more. It is increased consumption which induces
     higher investment, and in depressed times higher consumption
     levels are needed to induce greater output and increased
     investment.

....

Deflationary and Inflationary Gaps
The indicated equilibrium level of national income is not
necessarily a desirable level of economic activity. If the economy
is at full employment, and equilibrium is to the right or left of
this level, an inflationary or deflationary gap exists.

....

#4   A deflationary gap exists when consumption and investment

Figure 4.3

ASSIGNMENT 5   HS 304

SECTION IV   ECONOMICS

spending at full employment are less than the full employment national income level. At this level, scheduled saving is greater than scheduled investment. If investment does not increase to offset this difference, full employment cannot be maintained. Income will decrease and gravitate toward the indicated equilibrium.

....

#5   An inflationary gap, on the other hand, exists when consumption and investment spending at full employment is greater than full employment national income. In this case, scheduled saving is less than scheduled investment.

....

#6   Both gaps are measured at the full employment level. A deflationary gap is measured as the deficiency of full employment investment compared with full employment saving. The inflationary gap is measured as excess investment over saving at full employment. The vertical distance between the 45-degree line and the C + I schedule measures the gap.

....

#7   The C + I schedule will intersect the 45-degree line (equilibrium) to the left of full employment when the gap is deflationary, and to the right of full employment when the gap is inflationary.

....

#8   An inflationary gap is generally the result of demand-pull inflation. Demand-pull inflation is the type of inflation that occurs when too much purchasing power results in a demand for goods that exceeds the supply of goods that can be produced at full employment. In such a situation, buyers bid up the prices of goods. The new higher prices create higher incomes for businesses and wage earners which, in turn, generate more purchasing power, causing prices to spiral even further upward.

....

      Fiscal Policy
#9   Whenever a large inflationary or deflationary gap occurs, the government is called upon to use corrective measures to change the equilibrium level of income and close the gap. One form of

Figure 4.4

corrective measure used by government is called fiscal policy. This policy is used to raise or lower the equilibrium without inflation.

....

To illustrate the impact of fiscal policy, it is first necessary to complete the formula GNP = C + I by adding the G component.

....

#10 When government expenditures are added to consumption and investment spending, the new C + I + G schedule will intersect the 45-degree line at a new higher equilibrium level of national income. The new equilibrium, E_2, is to the right of E_1. At this new equilibrium level, total spending for goods equals the total income generated by producing the goods.

....

#11 If a deflationary gap exists, government will attempt to stabilize economic conditions through increased expenditures (G). When government expenditures are increased while all other factors remain constant, income not only rises, but in a multiplier way, because an increase in government expenditure has the same multiplier effect on income as does an increase in investment. Each new increase results in an upward shift of the C + I + G schedule, pushing national income to a new higher equilibrium level. Thus, increased government spending is one of the ways used to help close a deflationary gap. Another way is to decrease taxes. When all other factors are held constant, and only taxes are decreased, the initial result is increased disposable income. The increase in disposable income results in increased consumption, an upward shift in the C + I + G schedule, and consequently, an increased level of national income.

Government tax policies are also used to close an inflationary gap. In this case, taxes are increased while all other factors are held constant. Such an increase in taxes lowers disposable income, and consequently, lowers consumption spending. This shifts the C + I + G schedule downward to a new lower level of GNP.

....

Figure 4.5

ASSIGNMENT 5   HS 304

SECTION IV   ECONOMICS

....

The multiplier then acts only upon the change in consumption to reach the new national income level. Thus, it is essential that the marginal propensity to consume be known to calculate the impact on national income resulting from a change in taxes.

....

#12 A reduction of $20 billion in consumption will close the inflationary gap. Since MPC is 2/3, a tax increase of $30 billion will be needed to reduce consumption to the desired level.

....

#13 When MPC is 2/3, the full multiplier is 3.

The $20 billion increase in G is amplified by the multiplier, and national income is increased by $60 billion.

The $20 billion tax increase first reduces disposable income by that amount. The reduction in disposable income, with MPC = 2/3, results in a decrease of $13.33 billion in consumption. Applying the multiplier to this change results in a decrease of $40 billion in national income.

The net result of both actions is an increase of $20 billion in national income.

It is important to note that changes in taxes do not have the same full impact on national income as do changes in government expenditures. This results from the fact that taxation is not part of C + I + G, but that through disposable income, taxation has only an indirect influence on the level of national income. Disposable income includes consumption and saving, so part of the change in disposable income is saving, with the balance being consumption.

answers to such enabling questions are placed at the bottom of the page (or next page), rather than in the Summary. The rationale applied here is that the Summary is a summary of criterion objectives; to place all the enabling answers will only fragment the Summary, providing more details than necessary, and make the summary rather lengthy if many enabling questions were asked.

2. A second point to raise about the Summary is how to provide an answer to multiple-choice, matching, and similar kinds of discrimination-type questions. Answers to these types of questions, such as illustrated in Figure 3.5, are given both by the letter (or number) answer at the bottom of the page *and* by a written explanation in the Summary. The statement at the bottom of the page in Figure 3.5, *For Further Clarification Check Summary Item*, leaves an option open for the student who wants more details on the correct answer. This same procedure is highly useful for questions which have specific mathematical calculations, examples, or problem situations. The answer to the specific problem is given at the bottom of the page, while the general answer is referenced in the Summary. In following this procedure, the Summary is maintained as a summary as well as providing specific answers to criterion questions.

3. Note in the sample Summary that certain information is not blocked off; thus, it is not part of the answers. Several examples are shown in Figure 4.1, before and after the answer to question #1, and after the answer to question #2. This *information* is *connecting tissue*, so to speak, as it links confirmations to make a summary out of the series of individual answers. It is important to note that any information, outside a

blocked-off area, is only information. This cannot be instructional content which the student is expected to know as an objective, unless of course it was previously responded to. It is the *nice-to-know* or enrichment materials, but not content that is a part of an objective (again, unless previously learned). In essence, summary confirmations (in the blocked-off areas) are what the student *must* know, while the other is simply information. Without this connecting information, the answers as a summary might otherwise be read in a disjointed manner. However, there are times you will find that one answer can immediately follow another and the writer will have to be guided by what makes sense in making the answers fit together as a summary.

Cumulative Problem

Section V, Cumulative Problem, is an optional section that the designer may or may not want to include with the Adjunct Study Guide. It has a function similar to that of the Summary section, as a *summary*. As the title suggests, this section is intended to apply objectives together in a cumulative manner.

Often the objectives achieved in an assignment need to be or can be brought together for application to a common problem or series of problems. Figure 5.1 illustrates a problem that calls for application of several of the objectives learned in the assignment. Other examples might include a chemistry course lesson in which the cumulative objectives lead to an experiment, or a spelling improvement lesson on doubling final consonants before adding suffixes, that culminates in their application within sentences. Task-oriented lessons are common instances in which problems can be employed.

A second, common function of the cumulative problem is to provide practice analogous to a final examination. The student may well be expected, for example, to pass an achievement test for the entire course; and the cumulative problems in a series of lessons provide an excellent way to provide periodic checks on learning before the final examination. Corrective action by the student or teacher can then be planned and provided before this important phase of instruction is completed.

Generally, the cumulative problem is formulated to encompass as many as possible of the various aspects of the objectives learned in an assignment. These aspects of the objectives may be formulated on a generic or specific basis. Answers and explanations (as in Figure 5.2) of the cumulative problem are given immediately after the problem by a sample answer or checklist, and might include specific references in the answer to objectives covered.

The ASG Format

We can now summarize the design and operational use of the Adjunct Study Guide format. As noted earlier, student learning is guided from a general introductory level to specifics to a summary of the assignment or lesson. Two major sections are used for the introduction—the Purpose-Significance-Goals (Section I) and the Content Outline (Section II). Specific instruction is guided by the Objective-Reference-Question Section (III). The summary function is provided mainly by a Summary Section (IV), which may be augmented by other optional Sections, such as Cumulative Problems in the form of Cases, Experiments, Projects, and such.

The Purpose-Significance-Goals, Section I, introduces the student in a generic fashion to what the assignment or lesson will be concerned with and why it is important.

(text continued on page 58)

Figure 5.1

ASSIGNMENT 5 HS 304

SECTION V ECONOMICS

CUMULATIVE PROBLEM

"The concept of the multiplier is of more than theoretical interest. It not only helps us to explain why national income shifts up and down, instead of remaining constant or growing steadily, but is also is useful for governmental policy in times of economic depression."

(a)   Explain what is meant by the "multiplier" concept.

(b)   How does the multiplier concept help to explain "why national income shifts up and down?" Be specific.

(c)   By what reasoning might the author conclude that the multiplier concept can be "useful for governmental policy in times of economic depression"?

Figure 5.2

HS 304   ASSIGNMENT 5

ECONOMICS   SECTION V

SUGGESTED ANSWER TO CUMULATIVE PROBLEM

(a) The multiplier concept expresses the relationship between an increase in investment or government expenditures and the resulting increase in aggregate income. The size of the increase in income will depend upon the marginal propensity to consume. For example, if during a period of depression business decided to increase investment by $1,000,000, the recipients of this additional expenditure would spend a percentage of it (depending upon their marginal propensity to consume) on consumption goods. Those receiving income from the sale of consumption goods would in turn spend a percentage of it on consumption, and so on, with each succeeding recipient of income spending a portion of the new income. If we assume a constant marginal propensity to consume of, say, 80 percent of additional income in each succeeding spending period, a new investment of $1,000,000 will ultimately result in additional income of $5,000,000, or five times the original increment in investment.[4-13]

(b) The multiplier concept helps to explain fluctuations in national income by showing that relatively small changes in investment or government expenditures result in relatively large changes in national income because they are followed by changes in personal consumption expenditures. Such changes in personal consumption expenditures are in the same direction as the original changes in investment or government expenditures and thus magnify the latter's effect upon national income.

The operation of the multiplier concept may also be seen when a relatively small change in personal consumption expenditures—brought about by a change in taxes collected by the government or by a change in dividend policies of corporations—leads to a relatively large change in national income through subsequent changes in personal consumption expenditures in the same direction as the original change.[4-13]

....

4-13 See Assignment 4, Objective 13

Figure 5.2
(Continued)

(c) The multiplier concept can be "useful for governmental policy in times of economic depression" by indicating clearly that a given gap between the level of national income which the economy is capable of producing under conditions of full employment and the level of national income actually being produced may be closed by an increase in government expenditures and/or decrease in taxes only a fraction of the size of the gap. The remainder of the gap will be closed by subsequent increases in personal consumption expenditures brought about by the original increase in government expenditures and/or decrease in taxes.[11]

---

11 *See Objective 11*

The Content Outline, Section II, is an extension of Section I, designed to provide additional content orientation. The Outline may be used by the student as he or she proceeds through specific learner objectives in the next section, Objective-Reference-Questions.

In Section III, learning is guided by an objective by objective approach. The student reads a specific learner objective in context of the content heading from the Content Outline. Since the objective tells the student what he or she is to learn and how he or she will be expected to show mastery, the target of learning is clearly known as the student uses the Reference source(s) specified. Attention is then directed within the reading material (or other media sources) toward the objective. Notes may be taken for future reference within Section III. Having completed the use of Reference Sources, an opportunity is then provided to demonstrate mastery through questions directed at the objective. The correctness of the student's response to these questions can then be compared to representative answers provided in the fourth major section, the Summary. Not only does the Summary provide a means for comparative answers, but it also offers—upon completion of the study of all objectives—a means to tie the instruction together in a summary fashion. The use of the Summary for later review purposes is of particular value to the student. Finally, if applicable, a cumulative problem or series of problems is provided for purposes of combining objectives or as practice analogous to a final examination.

As a final note, directions on the instructional format and how it is to be used should be fully explained to the student(s) who will be using the ASG. To give the reader some idea of the kind of directions needed, the *Appendix* to this book contains the actual instructions given by the author to the students for whom he has designed and provided the ASG. With some minor modification, you may find the instructions of direct use in your own ASG designs.

IV.

OUTCOMES

As with any instructional design, outcomes to be expected should be viewed first in terms of what the design does for the student. The emphasis in discussing the Adjunct Study Guide is on use by the independent learner, and this emphasis should give some indication of what outcomes can be expected:

1. A much higher degree of learning effectiveness and efficiency should be achieved. Because most existing instructional materials, particularly textbooks, are non-interactive, learning effectiveness is not as great as it should be. The Adjunct Study Guide provides this necessary interaction, through active responding and confirmation. In addition, objectives pinpoint the learning targets more clearly for students, so that they can aim their reading, viewing, or listening at the *critical* content. Learning efficiency is achieved because specific references can be given to content, thus avoiding unnecessary or irrelevant content. When ineffective or deficient existing materials are found, they can be replaced by adding new materials to the study guide. Designers and teachers are often confronted with existing sources of instructional materials that do not quite match the students' instructional needs, but do contain the bulk of content, and thus the ineffective material is *put up with*. An adjunctive approach eases this problem.

2. A second outcome to be expected is that once the objectives of a lesson are achieved, they will be *seen in context*. The lesson is not learned as a set of isolated objectives. Rather, through that part of the Adjunct Study Guide design known as the Summary, provisions are made to review the individual objectives in relation to one another. This summary provision is particularly valuable with content that is cumulative in nature. In addition, students find the Summary quite valuable for review purposes after initial learning.

3. If the development of an Adjunct Study Guide is approached from the standpoint that its use will be by the independent studier, regardless of whether or not it will be augmented by subsequent in-class instruction, then a higher level of student preparation for in-class instruction can be expected. Therefore, classroom instruction becomes a time for meeting special learning problems. But will the students actually do the work outside of the class time? This question is easier to answer for college level study or job training programs than, say, for high school students. That is obvious and true enough. But consider this:

- If students know they have to use the study guide because that is the way you designed the course;
- If the content is *not* all going to be rehashed in class; and
- If they know that such instruction is effective and efficient for them;

Then the study guide will be used by the students. A good case can be made for the point of view that the reason students do not study outside class is not that they are lazy, but that they are given excuses not to study—and that the material given them lacks direction, objectives, and a real knowledge of *Am I learning?* An effective Adjunct Study Guide approach can help to take care of some of these doubts and problems. The reader may wish to review the *Construct Lesson Plan* instructional design, another book in this Series, as an effective classroom methodology for follow-up to the Adjunct Study Guide.

4. Finally, a real cost savings can be expected in terms of developmental time and use costs. Existing instructional materials constitute the bulk, if indeed not all of the content; thus, a lot of the instructional content need not be written anew. This saves development time, which means savings in production dollars.

V.

DEVELOPMENTAL GUIDE

Figure 6 represents a suggested order in which the various component parts of the Adjunct Study Guide might be developed. It is based on the developmental order in which the author has developed various instructional programs utilizing the ASG format. Following the guide is a brief descriptive account of the steps in more detail.

It is suggested that you briefly peruse the *Developmental Guide* before reading further. Note in particular any sequential steps which come at a point other than what you might have thought to be the case. Hopefully, the descriptive account will clarify why each step is suggested at the point in time that it is.

While a step by step procedure is given, it should be realized that many times these steps overlap and certain beginning points are stated before others are completely finished. Nonetheless, it is hoped that this guide will be of some assistance in your effort to develop the Adjunct Study Guide format for your own instructional needs.

Certain steps related to activities such as basic analysis for need and validation procedures have not been included, although they are important for overall effectiveness in program development. It is assumed that the reader would be aware of such needs.

Figure 6

Developmental Guide

	1	2	3	4	5	6	7	8
Assignment								
1. Objectives Written								
2. Criterion Questions and Answers Written								
3. Objectives and Questions Approved								
4. Sequence Objectives								
5. Existing References Specified to Objectives								
6. New Content Written								
7. Enabling Questions and Answers Written								
8. Sequence and Number 2, 5, 7 Above-Sec. III								
9. Sequence Criterion Question Answers								
10. Summary Written-Section IV Format								
11. Objective-Criterion Questions-Ans.-Summary Sequence Coding								
12. Content Outline Section II								
13. Cumulative Problem and Answers Written-Section V								
14. Purpose-Significance-Goals Finalized Section I								
15. Program Collated								
16. Program Completed								

Step 1

Assuming an instructional need has been determined to exist, program development normally begins with the specification of objectives. The reason is obvious. Simply put, it is difficult to know where one is going unless one states where he *intends* to go.

Step 2

The author finds it highly useful to write the questions and answers to the objectives immediately following the specification of the objectives. Such questions are confined at this point to those which will test the objective in their entirety (the criterion questions) rather than questions which might only help the students achieve the objectives (the enabling questions). The reasons for doing so are twofold. First, writing the criterion questions after the objectives provides details about the objectives. This is highly useful in determining what content resources will best suit the achievement of the objectives. In this regard, the criterion questions often help clarify the definition of the objectives, because the designer is forced to specify the means for the student to demonstrate to himself or herself that he or she has learned an objective.

The second reason for writing the criterion questions after the objectives, and not the enabling questions as well, is that writing the enabling questions would be a guessing exercise on the developer's part. Although the writing of enabling questions is suggested in Step 7, the author prefers to hold off on this effort until after the ASG program has been used by students for the first time. Objectives the students are unable to achieve with only the use of the objectives, resources, and criterion questions and answers can then be viewed for possible additions of enabling questions where actually needed. This helps avoid the guessing game of where enabling questions are properly needed and keeps the overall program *lean* and, thus, efficient.

Step 3

Approval of the Objectives and Questions is an administrative matter. Often as not, the development of an ASG, like most programs, is done on a cooperative basis among subject matter specialists or between a subject matter expert and a curriculum or instructional developer. This is a critical point for common agreement as to what the ends of learning are to be.

Step 4

The specifications drawn up in Steps 1 and 2 should provide sufficient information to determine a basic sequence of the objectives. While additional details from the reference sources (Step 5) may show where the sequence needs to be altered, the overall sequence by this step should be pretty well known. Actual use by students of the ASG may make for minor changes in the sequence at some future time, but an initial determination of sequence can be made at this early stage. This is particularly crucial for the eventual step of writing the Summary.

Step 5

While the specification of reference sources in most applications might well be restricted to one or two available sources, such as textbooks, consideration should extend where possible to other sources that might not seem so obvious. One of the sources the author has made use of is trade journals within the subject area of the course of study. Articles from a variety of weekly and monthly magazines have often proved useful, as have newspaper articles. Permission to reprint is generally an easy matter of writing to the publisher.

Of course, resource materials may be other than just printed matter. Guidance for what to use should be in accordance with availability and level of effectiveness in communicating to students. More than one source of content may be specified, with the option left to the student as to which and how much he or she might read, view, or see.

References sources can also include that which is specifically written by the developer of the ASG and included in either of two places. Lengthy content sources are generally recommended for placement at the end of an assignment. Shorter content sources, of a paragraph or two, may be placed immediately following the *reference* in Section III of the ASG, and are usually labeled *Content* or *Additional Content.*

The specification of references should generally be rather specific. Page numbers are preferred to chapter references, for instance. Even within such specific references, clarifying directions might indicate what need not be read, is accurate, or is out-of-date.

Finally, as a general rule, references need not, and usually are not, given according to the sequence of the reference source. One should recall that the sequence of learning has been determined in Step 4 above according to the best sequence of the objectives. This means, possibly, that the reference to pages in a textbook might well be other than the sequence of the textbook itself. This is one added advantage of an ASG approach.

Step 6

The need for writing new content sources has already been touched upon in Step 5. The reason for specifying this as a separate step is simply to point out that existing resources should be exhausted first for content that is effective, rather than immediately assuming that new content is needed. When and if new content is needed, it would be written or produced at this point in the total developmental effort.

Step 7
The specification of enabling questions and answers at this point in the developmental process has already been referred to as an activity that might be held off until after the ASG is used initially by a group of students. If, however, the developer deems it necessary to define and include some enabling questions and answers at this point in time, then it is suggested that such be done on a rather *lean* basis—that is, using as few such questions as would seem necessary. Prior experience in *known* areas of difficulty may suggest some points at which enabling questions would best be included.

Step 8
This step is an administrative one which pulls together the prior work completed in Steps 2, 5, and 7. In effect, Section III of the ASG is completed at this stage of development.

Step 9
Sequence the answers to the Criterion Question. This is a simple, preliminary, administrative procedure for what is to be accomplished in Step 10 which follows. Actually, the sequence has already been determined in Step 4, in that the objectives have already been sequenced. In the event the sequence as originally specified has changed, this step will remind the developers to be aware of this. Usually, the author accomplishes this step by placing the answers in the center of a blank 8½ x 11" paper; then, the *informational* content may be added before or after the specific answer in completing the function of writing the Summary (Step 10).

Step 10
As described in the *Design Format* part of this book, the

Summary is supposed to serve two functions. First, it is the source of answers to the Criterion Questions. Second, it is to be a coherent unit by itself which summarizes what has been learned and ties the learning objectives together. The latter function is achieved as well, one would hope, by the sequence of learning the objectives, although not probably as directly as the summary might achieve.

Writing the Summary is not a difficult task. After all, most of it has been written already by the answers to the criterion questions. These answers have been sequenced for their position in the Summary in Step 9 above. What remains is to write *information* that helps to tie the answers together. A good starting point in this regard is the placement of the answers under major and minor content headings. This gives some manageable sense of organization. Therefore, one may wish to complete Step 12 before writing the Summary, although the Content Outline in Step 12 is well known before one gets there.

Once the answers are organized within content headings, it simply remains a matter, from this point, of writing that which helps to join or provide a transition from one answer to another. Generally, this informational content is content you would not expect the students to know (simply because they haven't responded to it), although any content previously learned might be used. A careful inspection of the kind of content information used in the sample economics assignment Summary (Figures 4.1 through 4.5) should give you a better idea of what the nature of such *connecting* information is like. Note that sometimes one answer simply flows into the next without the necessity of connecting information, as illustrated by the answers numbered 5, 6, 7, and 9 of Figure 4.3. As a final comment, a good source of such connecting information is that which instructional designers often label as the *nice to know* content. Historical and enrichment content are generally two such kinds of *nice to know* content.

Step 11

Step 11 is an administrative consideration. The answers in the Summary must be identified by number to the questions for which they provide answers. Numbering the objectives from first to last, and then numbering the questions, as for instance questions 2.1, 2.2 to objective number 2, is a convenient system for numbering the answers in the Summary for easy location by the students. This step will complete Section IV of the ASG.

Step 12

Finishing the Content Outline (Section II) might, at this late stage, seem out of sequence for developmental purposes. To a certain degree, it is. The outline is really something the developer has in mind very early in the developmental process, most likely as early as determining the sequence of objectives in Step 4. Since the Summary in Step 10 needs content headings, the Outline is even more refined. In the opening remarks to the *Developmental Guide*, it was pointed out that some of these steps in the guide will overlap, and this is one step that certainly does overlap others. Nonetheless, it is at this point in the developmental process that the Content Outline can be finished. This completes Section II of the ASG.

Step 13

If Cumulative Problems or similar learning activities are to be included in the ASG, they can be developed at this point. The major aspects of the ASG have been completed and the designer is fully aware of what the assignment or lesson is concerned with and thus has a great deal of information on which to build other learning requirements which are to be included.

While many such requirements under this kind of cumulative study need to be viewed as part of a separate Section V of the ASG, it may well be that some of these would be more effectively studied and learned within the body of Section III. There is nothing to preclude the designer from including these at more appropriate points in Section III. For the sake of simplifying the discussion of the ASG, the author has chosen to describe these *cumulative study* needs as being separate.

Step 14

Again, this is a step, much like the Content Outline, which has its inception very early in the developmental effort. In fact, it is really the first step in the developmental effort. In a sense, it is merely typed at this stage. This completes Section I of the ASG.

Steps 15 and 16

These are merely administrative matters related to a final check of all the developmental effort accomplished in the previous steps.

VI.

RESOURCES

The Adjunct Study Guide is a relatively new instructional design, and as such you will find little additional reference and resources to which you might turn. However, some sources are available, and it is presupposed that the previous pages will suffice for the reader's needs. Sources which are available include:

BOOKS
Evans, Lionel and John Leedham. *Aspects of Educational Technology IX.* London, England: Kogan Page Limited, 1975.

Langdon, Danny G. *Interactive Instructional Designs for Individualized Learning.* Englewood Cliffs, N.J.: Educational Technology Publications, Inc., 1973.

ARTICLES
Langdon, Danny G. Confirmation Via (And A) Summary. *NSPI Journal,* September, 1970, 7-8, 14, and 17.

Langdon, Danny G. Instructional Designs for a Case Study Approach. *Educational Technology,* October, 1973, 51-54.

IN USE AT
Several of the courses of The American College currently use

the Adjunct Study Guide format. Descriptive information about these courses may be obtained from The American College, Bryn Mawr, Pa.

VII.

APPENDIX

How to Use the Study Guide

General Use

This Study Guide is truly a unique way to learn.

As shown in the Table of Contents, the Study Guide is divided into four major content divisions, encompassing fifteen assignments. Each assignment is subdivided into five sections, identified as follows:

SECTION I   Purpose, Significance, Goals,
                    and Text and Summary References

SECTION II   Outline of Subject Matter

SECTION III   Objectives and Questions

SECTION IV   Summary

SECTION V   Illustrative Objective and Essay
                   Questions and Answers

SECTION I has several parts. The *Purpose* outlines the importance of a particular assignment in the overall Economics Course. The *Significance* explains what you will learn and why you should learn it. Following these descriptions is a list of the *Goals*. The Goals specify the overall targets for the assignment achieved by working through the specific objectives. Finally, the *Text Reference* material you will be using for the assignment is specified and the first page of the Summary identified.

i

SECTION II, *Outline of Subject Matter*, lists the content for the assignment. It sets the stage for Section III by grouping the small areas of learning covered by specific objectives under larger topics. It is intended to give you an overall view of the assignment in terms of subject matter content.

SECTION III, *Objectives and Questions*, contains the specific objectives you are to learn grouped by topic. There may be as few as seven objectives or as many as twenty-two objectives in an assignment. Each objective unit is one page in length and subdivided into the following parts:

> TOPIC
> *Objective*
> *Reference*
> *Notes*
> *Question(s)*
> *Answer(s)*

You begin your study by reading the TOPIC and then the first *Objective* for that topic. This objective tells you precisely what content to learn and how you will be expected to demonstrate that you have learned that content. For example, a typical objective reads, *List and explain the three fundamental and interdependent economic problems facing any society.* This objective tells you what to learn, *the three fundamental and interdependent economic problems facing any society*, and also tells you how to demonstrate that you have learned, *list and explain*. For further details on the meaning of the various performance terms (i.e., *list*) for the objectives in this course, read pages iv and v.

The *Reference* part lists the specific source material you can use to study the objective. These references may include previous objectives, specific pages or tables in the textbook, or blocked-off material that will help clarify the resources that have been cited.

The *Notes* part is a space provided for you to write any notes you may wish to take, either from reading the reference sources or as a part of classroom discussion.

The *Question* part is a question, or series of questions, used to test your understanding and mastery of the objective you have been studying. In some instances the question is simply a restatement of the objective, while in other instances it might be a specific calculation or a situation to explain. The question is always in concert with the objective to be learned. You should *write* your answer to all questions and not just think them through. Writing an answer forces you to demonstrate what you have learned, and increases the probability that you will retain what you have learned.

The *Answer* part refers you to the Summary Item that is the correct answer to the question you have completed. These representative answers *should not be* viewed as a substitute for writing your own answer. Rather, each provides feedback on the correctness of your learning. After you have checked the correct answer in the Summary, you should return to Section III and study and answer the next objective.

SECTION IV, the *Summary*, has been designed to serve you in two ways. First, it contains the answers to the questions you completed in Section III. To find the answer to any specific question, simply locate the number in the left column of the Summary that corresponds with the number shown in the Answer part of Section III.

When you have completed *all* objectives for a given assignment, then the Summary can be used for its second purpose. That is, you can read the Summary in the same manner as you would a chapter summary in a book. This helps tie together all that you have been learning and also provides you with a valuable tool for later review purposes.

SECTION IV, the *Illustrative Objective and Essay Questions* are provided to test cumulative learning in preparation for the final examination. The answers to each question are also provided.

**Sample Use of the Study
Guide Sections**
The exhibits on pages vii through xii are samples of the five sections of an assignment. The Section number is located in the upper right or left hand corner of the page. You should follow these steps in using the Study Guide:

1. Read the Purpose, Significance, and Goals of Section I and have available the reference listed. Then read Section II, Outline of Subject Matter. For samples of these sections, see Exhibits 1 and 2 on pages vii and viii.
2. Go to Section III, begin with the first objective of that section, and proceed as follows: (for example, see Exhibit 3, page ix).
   A. Read the objective, noting carefully the specific content to be learned and the manner in which you will be expected to demonstrate that you have learned the content.

B. Read the reference material taking notes as you go.
C. Read the question and *write* your answer.
D. Compare your answer with the answer in Section IV, the Summary (see Exhibit 4).
3. Go back to the next objective in Section III and proceed as outlined above.
4. When you have completed all objectives, read Section IV, the Summary, from beginning to end. This will tie all the individual answers together (for sample, see Exhibit 4, page ix).
5. Go to Section V. Read the Illustrative Questions; *write* your answers; and then check your answers on the pages indicated, e.g., *see page 2.31* (for sample, see Exhibit 5, page xii).

Performance Terms

Each objective in this course is composed of two parts—a *description of the subject matter* and a *performance term*. The *description of subject matter* states the precise content to be learned. The *performance term* states the way to demonstrate that you have learned.

Performance terms include such action verbs as *explain, define, list, state, describe,* and so forth. The following is intended to serve as a guide to the meaning of some of the performance terms used in this course.

Performance Term		**Sample Objective**
DEFINE	Usually a very short statement describing the defining characteristics of a word or short statement.	Define the term *mixed economy.*
DESCRIBE	To give the *characteristics.* This includes the properties which distinguish it as being what it is.	Describe *specialization* and its relation to problems of alienation and interdependence.
DISTINGUISH	Usually qualified by another performance term (i.e., by definition). This means to	Distinguish between the *benefit* and *sacrifice* principles of taxation.

iv

describe, identify, etc., the essential differences between two or more objects, events, and so on. Has the same meaning as *contrast.*

EXPLAIN   To tell *why* an object, event, or circumstance is the way it exists or appears. This is sometimes asked in relation to some other set of circumstances, events or objects.

Explain how an *equilibrium system of prices and production* helps solve the three fundamental economic problems.

LIST   To write statements or words from memory, sometimes placing these in a given sequential order.

List five sources of U.S. federal taxes.

STATE   Usually to describe an object, event, or concept in very brief terms. Usually the recall of a very simple fact in nearly or exactly the same manner as learned.

State three ways in which the increasing role of government is reflected in the modern mixed economy.

CLU COURSE 8   ASSIGNMENT 2

ECONOMICS   SECTION I

Exhibit 1

Operation of the Mixed Economy

PURPOSE

The purpose of this assignment is to explain how the economy of the United States operates. Ours is a "mixed economy" in which both public and private institutions exercise economic control. Public economic influence and control has developed to counteract some of the competitive imperfections in our economy and to provide certain other benefits, such as social welfare. Some public control is exercised through the price system, and some is exercised in ways external to the price system. That government has an influence on economic life is widely accepted; what its objectives should be and its means for accomplishing them are the subject of much dispute.

SIGNIFICANCE

This assignment lays the foundation for an understanding of the choices among alternative policies and the impact of those policies. Specifically, this assignment discusses the nature of perfect and imperfect competition, the functioning of the price system, an historical perspective on government expenditure, and a survey of principles, problems, and policies of taxation.

GOALS

1. To appreciate the perfections and imperfections of a free enterprise system.
2. To understand the role government plays in counterbalancing the imperfections of free enterprise.
3. To understand the theory and operation of the tax system.

TEXT REFERENCES

Samuelson—Chapters 3, 8, and 9

Summary Begins on Page *2.25*

ASSIGNMENT 2   CLU COURSE 8

SECTION II   ECONOMICS

Exhibit 2

Outline of Subject Matter

1. The mixed economy (S 41-48)
   a. Perfect competition
   b. The price system
   c. Imperfections of competition

2. Capital, specialization, and money (S 49-55)
   a. Capital goods
   b. Capital and time
   c. Specialization, exchange, and division of labor
   d. Specialization and alienation
   e. Specialization and interdependence
   f. The use of money

3. Government participation in the economy (S 147-161)
   a. The growth of government participation in the economy
   b. The transfer expenditures of redistribution and personal income
   c. Government regulations and controls
   d. The changing functions of government
   e. The efficiency of government activity
   f. Justifiable government activities

4. Taxation (S 163-177)
   a. Principles of taxation
   b. Kinds of taxes
      i. Progressive, proportional, and regressive taxation
      ii. Direct versus indirect taxation
   c. Federal taxation
   d. The personal income tax
   e. State and local taxation
   f. Revenue sharing
   g. The incidence of taxation

CLU COURSE 8   ASSIGNMENT 2

ECONOMICS   SECTION III

Exhibit 3

Operation of the Mixed Economy

THE MIXED ECONOMY

#1   *Objective*   Define the term "mixed economy."

       Reference   Samuelson page 41

       Notes

       Question   What does the term "mixed economy" mean?

       Answer   CHECK SUMMARY ITEM #1

CLU COURSE 8   ASSIGNMENT 2

ECONOMICS   SECTION IV

Exhibit 4

Operation of the Mixed Economy

SUMMARY

#1   *The Mixed Economy*
A mixed economy is an economic system in which the questions of *what, how,* and *for whom* are decided partially by the free market and partially by a central government authority. In other words, a mixed economy is one in which both public and private institutions exercise economic control.

#2   Private institutions exercise economic control through a competitive system of prices and markets. In its most ideal form, this system results in "perfect competition"—situation in which no single entity (buyer or seller) controls a large enough share of the total market to influence market prices and quantities.

Under perfect competition, market price is determined through a system of trial-and-error. As consumer demand for a good rises, the price of that good also rises. At the higher price, more is produced, causing a rise in the demand for those factors needed in the production of that good. With the increase in supply, however, competitive pricing begins, causing the price of the good to fall. As the price falls, less is produced until both demand and supply are equal. Thus, through trial-and-error, an equilibrium of prices and production is reached.

#3   An equilibrium system of prices and production helps solve the three fundamental economic problems of *what, how* and *for whom.*

What goods are to be produced is determined by the interaction of consumer demand—the dollar votes of consumers as they

x

Exhibit 4
(Continued)

choose to purchase one item and not another—and business cost
and supply decisions made by producers. *How* goods are to be
produced is determined by the competition of producers.
Business firms try to adopt the least-cost combination of factor
inputs and the cheapest, most efficient methods of production.
For whom goods are to be produced is determined by the
distribution of income—the market supply and demand for
productive services.

....

These interactions should not be viewed as isolated decisions. It is
the combined interactions among all parts of the system which
help determine competitive equilibrium.

....

#4 In most situations, however, competition is not perfect. Imper-
fections arise because businessmen cannot predict changes in
consumer preferences. This results in . . .

ASSIGNMENT 2   CLU COURSE 8

SECTION V   ECONOMICS

Exhibit 5

Illustrative Objective Question

Which of the following is a progressive tax?

..... A.   The federal excise tax on gasoline

..... B.   State sales tax

..... C.   A 1½ percent city wage tax

..... D.   Real estate taxes

..... E.   Federal income tax

Answer   SEE PAGE 2.31

DANNY G. LANGDON is the Director of Instructional Design Research, The American College, Bryn Mawr, Pa. In his current capacity, Mr. Langdon conducts research to find more effective and efficient approaches to student learning. He has innovated several new approaches to learning, and is the founder of the *Zimdex* audio indexing system. Formerly a chemistry teacher in the U.S. Peace Corps and in public, secondary education in the U.S.A., Mr. Langdon gained much of his experience in developing and researching instructional programs in education and business through his work at General Programmed Teaching, Inc., Palo Alto, California, and the Parks Job Corps Center, Pleasanton, California. Mr. Langdon has contributed several articles and a book, plus conducted workshops in the general field of Instructional Technology.

D